Major European Union Nations

Major
European Union
Nations

Austria
Belgium
Czech Republic
Denmark
France
Germany
Greece
Ireland

Italy
The Netherlands
Poland
Portugal
Spain
Sweden
United Kingdom

Major European Union Nations

UNITED KINGDOM

by
Rae Simons and Shaina C. Indovino

Mason Crest

Mason Crest
370 Reed Road, Broomall,
Pennsylvania 19008
www.masoncrest.com

Printed in the Hashemite Kingdom of Jordan.

First printing
9 8 7 6 5 4 3 2 1

Library of Congress Cataloging-in-Publication Data

Simons, Rae, 1957-
   United Kingdom / by Rae Simons and Shaina C. Indovino.
      p. cm. — (The European union—political, social, and economic cooperation)
   Includes bibliographical references and index.
   ISBN 978-1-4222-2261-4 (hardcover) — ISBN 978-1-4222-2231-7 (series hardcover) — ISBN 978-1-4222-9276-1 (ebook)
   1. Great Britain—Juvenile literature. 2. Northern Ireland—Juvenile literature. 3. European Union—Great Britain—Juvenile literature. 4. European Union—Northern Ireland—Juvenile literature. I. Indovino, Shaina Carmel. II. Title.
   DA27.5.S56 2012
   941—dc22
                                        2010051852

Produced by Harding House Publishing Services, Inc.   914-2
www.hardinghousepages.com
Interior layout by Micaela Sanna.
Cover design by Torque Advertising + Design.

CONTENTS

United Kingdom

European Union Member since 1973

Scotland

Glasgow

Edinburgh

Tynemouth

Newcastle

Middlesbrough

Londonderry

Northern Ireland

Belfast

Kingston upon Hull

Leeds

Blackpool

Manchester

Liverpool

Sheffield

Dublin

Ireland

Nottingham

Leicester

Birmingham

Coventry

England

Cardiff

Bristol

London ✪

Chatham

Southampton

Brighton

Torbay

Plymouth

INTRODUCTION

Sixty years ago, Europe lay scarred from the battles of the Second World War. During the next several years, a plan began to take shape that would unite the countries of the European continent so that future wars would be inconceivable. On May 9, 1950, French Foreign Minister Robert Schuman issued a declaration calling on France, Germany, and other European countries to pool together their coal and steel production as "the first concrete foundation of a European federation." "Europe Day" is celebrated each year on May 9 to commemorate the beginning of the European Union (EU).

The EU consists of twenty-seven countries, spanning the continent from Ireland in the west to the border of Russia in the east. Eight of the ten most recently admitted EU member states are former communist regimes that were behind the Iron Curtain for most of the latter half of the twentieth century.

Any European country with a democratic government, a functioning market economy, respect for fundamental rights, and a government capable of implementing EU laws and policies may apply for membership. Bulgaria and Romania joined the EU in 2007. Croatia, Serbia, Turkey, Iceland, Montenegro, and Macedonia have also embarked on the road to EU membership.

While the EU began as an idea to ensure peace in Europe through interconnected economies, it has evolved into so much more today:

• Citizens can travel freely throughout most of the EU without carrying a passport and without stopping for border checks.

• EU citizens can live, work, study, and retire in another EU country if they wish.

• The euro, the single currency accepted throughout seventeen of the EU countries (with more to come), is one of the EU's most tangible achievements, facilitating commerce and making possible a single financial market that benefits both individuals and businesses.

• The EU ensures cooperation in the fight against cross-border crime and terrorism.

• The EU is spearheading world efforts to preserve the environment.

• As the world's largest trading bloc, the EU uses its influence to promote fair rules for world trade, ensuring that globalization also benefits the poorest countries.

• The EU is already the world's largest donor of humanitarian aid and development assistance, providing around 60 percent of global official development assistance to developing countries in 2011.

The EU is not a nation intended to replace existing nations. The EU is unique—its member countries have established common institutions to which they delegate some of their sovereignty so that decisions on matters of joint interest can be made democratically at the European level.

Europe is a continent with many different traditions and languages, but with shared values such as democracy, freedom, and social justice, cherished values well known to North Americans. Indeed, the EU motto is "United in Diversity."

Enjoy your reading. Take advantage of this chance to learn more about Europe and the EU!

Ambassador John Bruton,
Former EU President and Prime Minister of Ireland

London's skyline.

CHAPTER 1

MODERN ISSUES

Mae-Ann Smith lives in the United Kingdom (UK), one of Europe's oldest nations, and a founding member of the European Union (EU). The lands that make up the UK—England, Scotland, Wales, and Ireland—are lands of legend with long histories of pride and dignity. But Mae-Ann doesn't feel she has a part of the UK's long legacy of freedom and human rights. Even though she's lived in the UK her entire life, she still feels like an outsider.

THE FORMATION OF THE EUROPEAN UNION

The EU is a confederation of European nations that continues to grow. All countries that enter the EU agree to follow common laws about foreign security policies. They also agree to cooperate on legal matters that go on within the EU. The European Council meets to discuss all international matters and make decisions about them. Each country's own concerns and interests are important, though. And apart from legal and financial issues, the EU tries to uphold values such as peace and solidarity, human dignity, freedom, and equality. All member countries remain autonomous. This means that they generally keep their own laws and regulations. The EU becomes involved only if there is an international issue or if a member country has violated the principles of the union.

The idea for a union among European nations was first mentioned after World War II. The war had devastated much of Europe, both physically and financially. In 1950, French foreign minister Robert Schuman suggested that France and West Germany combine their coal and steel industries under one authority. Both countries would have control over the industries. This would help them become more financially stable. It would also make war between the countries much more difficult. The idea was interesting to other European countries as well. In 1951, France, West Germany, Belgium, Luxembourg, the Netherlands, and Italy signed the Treaty of Paris, creating the European Coal and Steel Community. These six countries would become the core of the EU.

In 1957, these same countries signed the Treaties of Rome, creating the European Economic Community. This combined their economies into a single European economy. In 1965, the Merger Treaty brought together a number of these treaty organizations. The organizations were joined under a common banner, known as the European Community. Finally, in 1992, the Maastricht Treaty was signed. This treaty defined the European Union. It gave a framework for expanding the EU's political role, particularly in the area of foreign and security policy. It would also replace national currencies with the euro. The next year, the treaty went into effect. At that time, the member countries included the original six plus another six who had joined during the 1970s and '80s.

In the following years, the EU would take more steps to form a single market for its members. This would make joining the union even more of an advantage. Three more countries joined during the 1990s. Another twelve joined in the first decade of the twenty-first century. As of 2012, six countries were waiting to join the EU.

Europe is proud of its "bright idea," a union with economic and political power.

Traveler History

After the bombs of World War II, many people were left homeless in the UK. Traveler groups absorbed thousands of these individuals into their communities. Today, in the United Kingdom, the Gypsy and Traveler community is made up of people of Roma descent, along with Irish Travelers and other Traveler groups. UK officials estimate that 90,000 to 120,000 Gypsies and Travelers still live the traditional nomadic life in their country, while another 200,000 have been forced to settle down and live in permanent housing of some form. Their exact numbers are hard to determine for certain, since they are not recorded on UK census records.

The Roma and Other Travelers

Mae-Ann lives in a trailer. (In the rural English village where Mae-Ann lives, the trailer is called a caravan). She lives there not because she can't afford a house, but because, for Mae-Ann, living in a trailer is an **affirmation** of her cultural identity. She and her people are not House-Dwellers. They're Travelers.

You may have never heard of Mae-Ann's people. If you have, you may think of them as Gypsies. Some people call them Roma. People have hated and feared them for centuries. Mae-Ann has faced *racism* her entire life.

But being a Traveler is still important to Mae-Ann. It's who she is, it's who her parents were, and it's who she wants her children to be. But she hates the fact that people hate her and her children simply because of who they are.

"Some people choose to live on the farmland they inherited from their families versus moving to the city," she said. "They want to live close to the land and keep their lifestyle simple. What if those people were hated and looked down on, simply because of how and where they choose to live? No one does that, of course. But they don't see that how they treat the Roma is the same thing."

Mae-Ann explains that the laws in the United Kingdom have made it difficult for her people to live their traditional lifestyle. "We can't move around anymore like we used to. Now there are laws that say we can't set up our camps on the land where we always did. So we're forced to either break the law—or buy land and set up permanent camps. But even then, towns don't want us. They tell us we can't live here. They take advantage of loopholes in the law and push us out. What are we supposed to do? They want to destroy us, so we don't know who we are anymore.

"My daughter has blonde hair. You can't tell by looking at her that she's Gypsy. What makes her different is that she's not a House-Dweller. I want her to know who she is. I want her to live with her people. But people around here don't want that. So I have to choose—do I want my daughter to grow up knowing who she is? Or do I want her to grow up being accepted by the other children in her school? I shouldn't have to make that choice. But my

WHO ARE THE ROMA?

About a thousand years ago, groups of people migrated from northern India, spreading across Europe over the next several centuries. Though these people actually came from several different tribes (the largest of which were the Sinti and Roma), the people of Europe called them simply "Gypsies"—a shortened version of "Egyptians," since people thought they came from Egypt.

Europeans were frightened of these dark-skinned, non-Christian people who spoke a foreign language. Unlike the settled people of Europe, the Roma were wanderers, with no ties to the land. Europeans did not understand them. Stories and stereotypes grew up about the Gypsies, and these fanned the flames of prejudice and discrimination. Many of these same stories and stereotypes are still believed today.

Throughout the centuries, non-Gypsies continually tried to either assimilate the Gypsies or kill them. Attempts to assimilate the Gypsies involved stealing their children and placing them with other families; giving them cattle and feed, expecting them to become farmers; outlawing their customs, language, and clothing, and forcing them to attend school and church. In many ways the Roma of Europe were treated much as the European settlers treated the Native peoples of North America.

Many European laws allowed—or even commanded—the killing of Gypsies. A practice of "Gypsy hunting"—similar to fox hunting—was both common and legal in some parts of Europe. Even as late as 1835, a Gypsy hunt in Denmark "brought in a bag of over 260 men, women, and children." But the worst of all crimes against the Roma happened in the twentieth century, when Hitler's Third Reich sent them to concentration camps. As many as half a million Gypsies died in the Nazis' death camps.

Today the EU has passed laws that protect the Roma's right—but many of the EU's member nations struggle with those laws. Prejudice and discrimination against the Roma and other Travelers is a big problem in the EU.

people and I aren't welcome in this country. We're not welcome anywhere. We've been hated and driven out for the last thousand years."

Mae-Ann isn't exaggerating her situation. Her story is being acted out again and again across the United Kingdom. For instance, the residents of one English village built walls of concrete blocks and mud to keep Gypsies from the land they had bought for their caravans.

The group of Travelers had bought the field at the edge of town in 2001. They'd put in water and electricity, built cement foundations for their caravans, and created driveways. By the next year, twenty-some families were living there. They thought they'd done everything right. They didn't realize they had failed to submit one essential piece of paperwork to the town government.

In 2004, the town's **bailiffs**, backed by a hundred police officers, forced the community's residents out of their homes. Townspeople got involved; fights broke out; people were injured; and one caravan was set on fire and destroyed.

"The families who were here have been traveling around the country just trying to find somewhere to stay," a member of the Gypsy Council told a BBC reporter. "If people can't live on their own land they end up living illegally on other people's plots or illegally by the road side."

Of course, each story always has two sides. The village government insisted its actions had nothing to do with **discrimination**, that it was merely applying a law that protects rural landscapes from development. The townspeople supported this view. They did not want the Gypsy community in their village because of the noise, illegal dumping, and vandalism the Gypsies brought with them (according to the villagers). When a BBC reported asked a resident if he had actually met any of the **evicted** Gypsies, he responded, "Are you serious? They were just not normal. Clash of cultures has nothing to do with it. If anyone had 15 families moving next door to them they would feel **intimidated**." The local authorities also claimed that they'd already done their part on behalf of Gypsies: the village has an existing, approved Travelers' caravan not far from the illegal site.

When you walk through this official site, you find a well-kept trailer park that's home to ten families. All the plots are taken, and no one sounds like they're planning to move, so clearly, this site will do the evicted Gypsies no good. The residents say their kids attend the local schools, and they don't want to move for fear they won't find anywhere else to "stop" legally. The residents also say they try not to draw attention to themselves. One resident told the BBC reporter, "The [villagers] may talk about [garbage dumping] from the other community but our experience is different. I have been woken up by cars from who knows where emptying rubbish on to our back field. Who do you think gets the blame?"

"This just the way it goes if you're a Traveler," Mae-Ann said. "You don't even feel surprised or outraged when you hear stories like this. It's just what you expect. And I think that's the saddest thing—that we just take it, that we accept it, like it's a fact of life we can't change."

Mae-Ann Smith is clearly an angry woman, but her anger makes her sad. "Does anyone remember that half a million Gypsies were killed by the Nazis during World War II? No. People remember the Jews. People feel like the world owes the Jews for looking away when that terrible thing was happening. But no one feels like the world owes the Gypsies anything. Today, Gypsies face more prejudice than any other group in Europe. It's true. Some people hate the Arabs, or others look down on people with black skin—but almost everyone hates Gypsies. No one wants us in their community. Everyone thinks they're right to not want us around. They think, 'I'm not prejudiced because Gypsies really are nuisances no one would want in their community

Roma often end up living in trailer parks such as these in the United Kingdom.

Mae-Ann waved her hand at the electric plant squatting next door to the park where she lives. "See that? The legal sites we're given are always next to things like that. Or next to railroad tracks, or in the middle of an industrial site. Places where no one else would want to live. Places that are dangerous for our children, for our health."

The UK prides itself on its tolerance and respect for human rights—and yet people like Mae-Ann know that discrimination and prejudice exist even in a modern enlightened nation like the UK. Meanwhile, other groups of people within the UK are also struggling to be accepted.

IMMIGRATION

Immigration is another issue the UK is facing in the twenty-first century. One of the Four Freedoms of the EU is the right for people to pass back and forth across nations' borders within the EU's members. This means that people from other countries have a legal right to move to the UK. Since the

The EU's united economy has allowed it to become a worldwide financial power.

expansion of the EU on May 1, 2004, the UK has accepted immigrants from Central and Eastern Europe, Malta, and Cyprus. Immigrants from Poland have become especially common.

Immigration is a fact of life throughout the EU, with people moving from the poorer member nations to those that are wealthier and more stable. Not everybody is happy about this, though. People worry that with so many people coming to Western Europe (including the UK), there will not be enough jobs to go around. They worry that the government will not have enough money to take care of everyone.

Experts, however, point out that immigrant workers have actually helped improve worker wages in the UK. Most of the UK's immigrants are hard workers who end up paying more in taxes than they receive in welfare payments.

As a result of immigrants' presence, the UK is becoming increasingly multicultural. Some people feel worried that their nation will lose its traditional way of life—but many British people welcome the contributions immigrants bring to their country.

FINANCIAL ISSUES

One of the issues affecting the UK is the **recession** that hit the entire world in 2008. Like the other nations in the EU, the UK is struggling to get back on its feet financially. Things have improved in the UK, but there are still problems to be faced. **Inflation** is high, while wages often remain low; this means that people have less money to spend. It's a particularly difficult situation for people who are retired and are living on a fixed-income. While things cost more, their **pensions** stay the same, which makes it hard for them to make ends meet.

When people are anxious about their jobs and their futures, when they're worried about whether they will be able to pay for the things they need in their lives, they often become tense and stressed. It may be more difficult for them to feel tolerant of other groups of people, such as the Roma and immigrants.

But despite these issues, the UK continues to be a strong nation. That strength is built on a long, proud history.

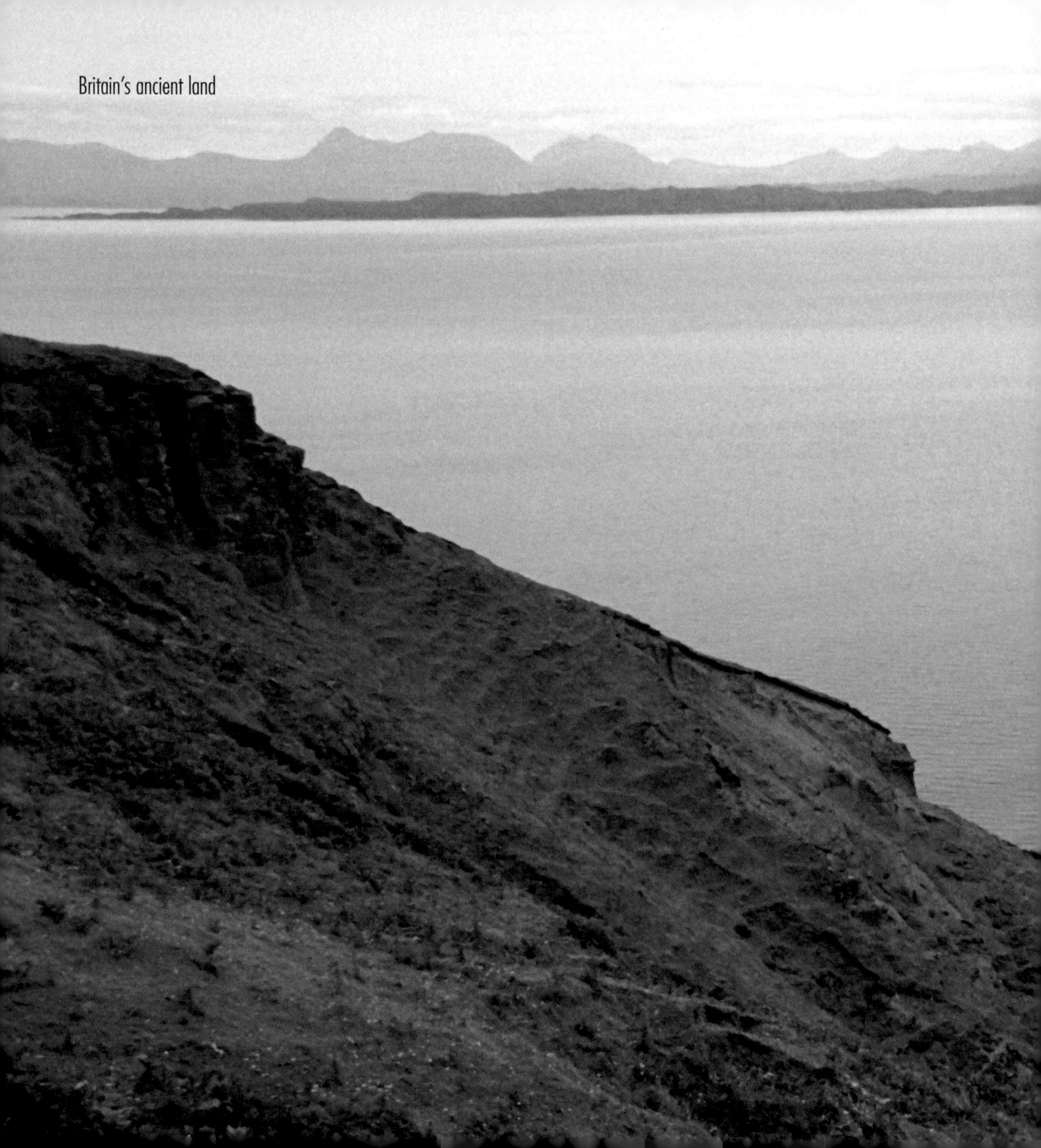

2 CHAPTER BRITAIN'S ANCIENT HISTORY AND MODERN GOVERNMENT

Almost everyone has heard of King Arthur and his knights . . . Robin Hood . . . the Loch Ness Monster . . . Shakespeare . . . and pixies and brownies. These characters from history, literature, and mythology have helped shape the world's imagination. The roots of these stories are all deep in Britain's ancient soil.

More than two and a half million years ago, the first Stone-Age people settled the land that is now the United Kingdom. At that time, however, the land was not an island; the British Islands were not separated from the rest of Europe until 8,500 years ago, when melting glaciers formed the English Channel that today separates England from France.

About three thousand years after Britain became an island, new tribes came by boat from the mainland. They built forts and tombs made of earth; many of these ancient manmade hills and mounds can still be seen across the British Isles.

Centuries later, when Britain's climate abruptly became both colder and wetter, its inhabitants moved down from the higher grounds to the lowlands, About five hundred years later, a new wave of immigrants—the Celts—started to arrive from southern Europe. They may have brought with them a new technology: ironworking.

Historians don't know very much about these half-forgotten people. What they do know comes from information archeologists have pieced together from the objects left behind by Britain's first people. Not until more than two thousand years after Stonehenge's first stones were erected, did someone come to the British Isles who could read and write: Pytheas, a Greek who traveled there around 330 BCE. Most of Pytheas's writings have been lost, so the first written records we have of Britain are when the Romans arrived, almost three hundred years after Pytheas.

THE ROMAN INVASION

In 55 BCE, Julius Caesar's troops invaded the British Isles. Caesar was hoping to gain gold, silver, and tin from Britain, but victory did not come easily. Although his well-trained armies did win some battles, the wild seas around the islands protected them well, and again and again, Caesar's ships were wrecked by storms.

Not until a century later, in 43 CE, did the Romans manage to bring the British Isles into their empire. This time the Roman emperor sent 40,000 soldiers, some of them mounted on elephants. The British had never seen such animals, and they were terrified!

For almost four hundred years—nearly twice as long as the United States has been a nation—the Roman Empire ruled Britain. During that time, Britain had more

STONEHENGE

About 4,500 years ago, the same people who built earthworks across Britain learned to build stone monuments. The most mysterious and imposing is Stonehenge, a circle of enormous stones that is probably the world's most famous prehistoric construction. For centuries, Stonehenge has fascinated people from around the world, and many theories have been created about why it was built. Some say it was the site of ancient astronomy, while others surmise that it was connected to long-ago religious beliefs—but no one knows for sure why or how it was built.

The mysterious stones of Stonehenge

Ancient ruins attest to Wales' long history.

contact with the rest of Europe than it had ever had before. The Romans' stable government brought peace and culture. The Romans also built a system of roads, many of which are still in use. The remains of their buildings and baths can be seen across the United Kingdom.

But no empire lasts forever, and in 410 CE, the weakened Roman Empire withdrew from Britain. The peaceful inhabitants who remained behind were left with no strong army to protect them.

WAS THERE REALLY A KING ARTHUR?

Most people have heard the legends that surround King Arthur—but not everyone knows that these stories may contain elements of actual history. Geoffrey of Monmouth, a Welsh monk who lived in the twelfth century, wrote a book called *The History of the Kings of Britain*, where he identified Arthur as a high king from Britain's ancient past. In his book, Geoffrey placed Arthur's life in a span of time ranging from the late fifth century to 542, during the years when Rome had withdrawn from the British Isles, leaving behind political chaos and lawlessness. Geoffrey claimed to have based his work on a "certain very ancient book written in the British language." Historians today can only surmise how much of Geoffrey's story was based on truth and how much he made up. In any case, the story he wrote became the basis of the Arthurian legend that later made its way into the collective imagination of the English-speaking world.

THE INVASION OF THE ANGLO-SAXONS

The tribes of Denmark, northern Germany, and Holland (called the Angles, the Jutes, and the Saxons) realized that the islands were vulnerable. Their own land was poor and often flooded, and they were looking for new places to live and farm. Anglo-Saxon families rowed across the North Sea in wooden boats and formed small settlements on Britain's land. Eventually, they ruled most of Britain, although they never conquered Wales and Cornwall in the west or Scotland in the north. The Anglo-Saxon king, Alfred the Great, was the first ruler to control most of England. In 597 CE, St. Augustine came to Britain as a missionary from Rome, and the Anglo-Saxons gradually converted to Christianity.

THE NORMANS

For centuries, Vikings had been sweeping down from the north to raid the European lands to the south. Britain bore its share of these raids, as did France across the English Channel. Around 1000 CE, a group of Vikings—called "North Men" or "Normans"—settled in France in the area that is now known as Normandy. The Normans became Christians, but as the generations passed, some of them grew tired of farming and wanted the adventures and riches of their grandfathers.

ROBIN HOOD

According to legend, the folk hero was a good-hearted outlaw who lived in England's Sherwood Forest during the rule of King John, "robbing from the rich and giving to the poor." Much like King Arthur, Robin is a legendary figure who may have been based on a real person or persons. One of the most likely candidates is Robyn Hood who served as a porter to the king's court between March 24 and November 22, 1324. Some historians speculate that Robyn Hood is the same person as Robert Hood, a tenant of Wakefield, Yorkshire, who appears in records in 1316. (Wakefield is only ten miles [16 kilometers] from Barnsdale, the medieval home of the legendary Robin Hood.) What's more, Robert's wife was named Matilda, Maid Marian's true name in Elizabethan plays. Robert, like the legendary Robin Hood, may also have been the son of a forester named Adam.

In 1066, William, Duke of Normandy, sailed across the English Channel and conquered the Anglo-Saxons. William became the new king of England. He built many castles, where his **nobles** lived, and he made French the official language. For many years, both French and Anglo-Saxon were spoken across Britain. (The English that is spoken today, however, has more roots in Anglo-Saxon than it does in French.) William the Conqueror, as well as his son and grandson, were strong kings who once again brought a stable government to Britain.

William the Conqueror's great-grandson, King John, however, did not get along well with the nobles. In 1215, they rebelled and forced him to sign the Magna Carta—Latin for "Great Charter"—a document that would form the foundation for Britain's (and later, Canada's and America's) government.

THE RISE OF THE TUDORS

In the fifteenth century, **civil wars** called the Wars of the Roses threatened to tear apart Britain's peaceful countryside. A white rose was the badge of the Yorkists, while their opponents, the Lancastrians, wore a red rose as their symbol. Both sides' leaders had royal blood, and both claimed the throne. Across Britain, the nobles took one side or another, and battles raged for thirty years. The fighting finally ended in 1485 when the York king was defeated. A Welshman, Henry VII, the first of the line of kings called the Tudors, took the throne and brought peace back to Britain.

Henry's son was Henry VIII, famous both for his many wives and for starting the Anglican Church, which still exists. After his death, his daughter Elizabeth eventually took the throne, becoming one of England's greatest monarchs. During her reign, Britain's power grew, and its influence extended across the seas, all the way to North America, where her adventurers sailed. Because Elizabeth never married, she was known as the Virgin Queen; the American state of Virginia was named after her.

These were eventful years in Britain's history. During the reign of Elizabeth's cousin James, in 1620, the Pilgrims set sail for New England aboard

Medieval castle overlooking Edinburgh in Scotland

Wales looks out toward the mysterious West.

the *Mayflower*. As Britain's power at home grew, its people also traveled far across the ocean and began settling the "New World." Kings came and went, while the British people prospered, both on their island home and across the oceans in their many colonies around the world.

THE VICTORIAN AGE

By the nineteenth century, Britain had formed an **empire**. So many British colonies were spread around the globe that people said: "The sun never sets on the British Empire." In other words, somewhere on the globe, the sun was shining on one British colony or another. Although the American colonies were now their own nation, Canada,

DID THE WELSH DISCOVER AMERICA?

Did you know that Madoc, a Welsh prince, is said to have discovered America in the twelfth century, long before Columbus? According to Welsh legend, Madoc sailed westward with a group of followers, seeking lands far away from the constant warfare of his native Wales. The story goes that his eight ships made landfall in 1169, at what is now called Mobile Bay, Alabama. Liking what he found, Madoc then returned to Wales for additional settlers; in 1171, the courageous little band sailed away and was never heard from again—at least in Europe. But tradition has it that Madoc and his followers settled in the Mississippi Valley, intermarrying with the Natives, whom they showed how to build the stone forts that remain in the area. The legend of Madoc (or Madog, as he is called sometimes) played a role in both English and American history. Many historians now dismiss it as more fancy than fact—and yet it may very well contain some element of truth.

THE GREATEST AUTHOR IN THE WORLD

The arts flourished during Elizabeth's peaceful reign. One of the most famous writers of all times—William Shakespeare—lived during the time Elizabeth was queen. Shakespeare's mastery of the English language has never been surpassed, and his plays and poetry continue to be enjoyed by people around the world.

Australia, New Zealand, India, and much of Africa and the Middle and Far East were all part of this far-spread empire.

Queen Victoria ruled during these years of British power and influence. She took the throne in 1837, when she was only eighteen, and she reigned for more than sixty-three years, longer than any other British king or queen. Her personality shaped not only Britain but the entire world.

A quarter of the entire world's population lived under Victoria's rule, and she built Britain into the greatest trading empire the world had ever known. The empire's administrators genuinely believed they were helping the people they ruled; they abolished slavery throughout their colonies and brought education, law, democracy, and sports to the countries they governed. The native people of

THE HISTORY AND GOVERNMENT OF WALES

For centuries, Wales was an independent kingdom that resisted English rule, a Celtic stronghold ruled by sovereign princes. In 1282, however, King Edward I brought Wales under English rule. Edward's eldest son was born in Wales in 1284 and became the first English Prince of Wales in 1301. The eldest son of the reigning monarch continues to bear this title; Prince Charles is the modern-day Prince of Wales.

At the beginning of the fifteenth century, the Welsh revolted against unjust English laws, but their rebellion failed. The Tudor dynasty, which was of Welsh ancestry, ruled England from 1485 to 1603, and during this period the Acts of Union (1536 and 1542) united England and Wales administratively, politically, and legally. Wales nationalism has never died, however, and in July 1999, a National Assembly for Wales was given specific powers to make legislation to meet Welsh needs.

THE TWENTIETH CENTURY

By the time of Queen Victoria's death in 1901, other nations, including the United States, had developed their own manufacturing factories. Although Britain was a world leader during the battles of World War I, the war's losses and destruction, combined with the **Depression** of the 1930s, eroded the United Kingdom's international leadership.

At the same time, Britain's control over its empire loosened during the years between the world wars. Ireland, with the exception of six northern counties, gained independence from the United Kingdom in 1921. **Nationalism** became stronger in other parts of the empire, especially in India and Egypt.

the colonies, however, were not always grateful, and historians still debate whether the British Empire was good for its colonies.

During Victoria's years on the throne, Britain was a leader in the Industrial Revolution. Goods that were once made by hand were now made in factories by machines. More and more people moved away from their farms and turned to the cities for jobs. London became the largest city in the world. Britain was the manufacturing leader of the world—but its workers paid the price with terrible living and working conditions.

Although Queen Victoria had tremendous influence, Parliament was actually in charge of the country during her reign, and British citizens gained most of the rights of democracy. Working people began fighting for better conditions and more fair pay.

CHARLES DICKENS

English author Charles Dickens wrote during the Industrial Revolution, exposing some of the evils that poor people endured during this era. Some of his most famous characters are Ebenezer Scrooge (a miserly rich man haunted by the ghosts of Christmas) and Oliver Twist (a poor orphan living on the streets of London).

The wild and ancient kingdom of Wales

Edinburgh, Scotland's capital city, is a mixture of old and new.

In 1926, the United Kingdom granted Australia, Canada, and New Zealand complete **autonomy** within the empire. These nations be-came **charter members** of the British Commonwealth of Nations (now known as the Commonwealth). Beginning with the independence of India and Pakistan in 1947, the remainder of the British Empire was almost completely dismantled. Today, most of Britain's former colonies belong to the Commonwealth, almost all of them as independent members. However, thirteen former British colonies—including Bermuda, Gibraltar, the Falkland Islands, and others—have chosen to continue their links with the United Kingdom; they are known as United Kingdom Overseas Territories.

During World War II, Britain fought heroically against the **Axis** forces, but the war took a heavy toll on British cities, resources, and human life. Great Britain's culture was forever changed. When the war was finally over, the British people voted for a Labour government, and the National Health Service was introduced. This gave free health care to everyone, paid for by people's taxes.

SCOTLAND'S HISTORY AND GOVERNMENT

Evidence of human settlement in what is now Scotland dates back five thousand years. By the time the Romans invaded Britain, many tribes were living in the region. Despite attempts to control these tribes, Roman rule never permanently extended to most of Scotland. The kingdoms of England and Scotland were frequently at war during the Middle Ages (1000–1400 CE). When King Edward I tried to impose direct English rule over Scotland in 1296, a revolt for independence broke out; it ended in 1328, when King Edward III officially recognized the rebellion's leader, Robert the Bruce, as King Robert I of Scotland.

While maintaining separate parliaments, England and Scotland were ruled under one crown beginning in 1603, when James VI of Scotland succeeded his cousin Elizabeth I as James I of England. In the century that followed, strong religious and political differences divided the kingdoms. Finally, in 1707, England and Scotland were unified as Great Britain, sharing a single Parliament at Westminster. Nearly three hundred years later, in July 1999, power to administer Scottish affairs was given to a new Scottish assembly.

Today, the United Kingdom's major political parties are Labour and Conservative. Margaret Thatcher, who led the Conservative Party, became Britain's first-ever woman prime minister in 1979. She was prime minister until 1990. John Major followed her, and in 1997, Tony Blair was elected; in 2007, Gordon Brown became prime minister; and in 2010, David Cameron became the prime minister of the United Kingdom.

All through the twentieth century, Britain was America's closest ally, and that partnership contin-

Big Ben, near England's Parliament buildings

ues into the twenty-first century. Troops from the two countries worked together to overthrow Saddam Hussein, and they continued to work to stabilize Iraq.

THE UNITED KINGDOM'S GOVERNMENT

The United Kingdom does not have a written constitution. Instead, its government is based on **common law** and "traditional rights."

Changes may come about formally through new acts of Parliament, informally through the acceptance of new practices and usage, or by judicial precedents. Although Parliament has the theoretical power to make or repeal any law, in actual practice the weight of seven hundred years of tradition acts as a restraint against any **arbitrary** actions.

Executive government rests in name only with the monarch; actually, it is controlled by a committee of ministers (a cabinet) traditionally selected

IRELAND'S HISTORY AND GOVERNMENT

Ireland's invasion by the Anglo-Normans in 1170 led to centuries of unrest as one English king after another sought to conquer Ireland. In the early seventeenth century, large-scale settlement of the north from Scotland and England began. In the years that followed, Ireland was subjected, with varying degrees of success, to control and regulation by Britain.

The legislative union of Great Britain and Ireland was completed on January 1, 1801, under the name of the United Kingdom. The question of Home Rule for Ireland, however, remained one of the major issues of British politics. In 1919, the Irish Republican Army (IRA) began operations against the British administration, and in 1920, a new Government of Ireland Act provided for separate parliaments in Northern and Southern Ireland (both operated under control of Britain's Parliament). The act was implemented in Northern Ireland in 1921, giving six of the nine counties of the province of Ulster their own Parliament with powers to manage internal affairs. However, the act was not accepted in the south, and in 1921, the twenty-six counties of southern Ireland left the United Kingdom, while the six northern, predominantly Protestant counties remained part of the United Kingdom.

From 1921 until 1972 Northern Ireland had its own Parliament. In the late 1960s and early 1970s, the civil rights movement and reactions to it led to rioting, and the British Army was sent in to help the police keep law and order. Terrorism and violence continued to increase, and in 1972, the United Kingdom decided to take back direct responsibility for Ireland's law and order. The Irish Northern Ireland Unionist government resigned in protest; the regional government was abolished, and direct rule from England began. This lasted until powers were given back to a Northern Ireland Assembly in December 1999.

London's Parliament buildings

THE HISTORY AND GOVERNMENT OF THE CHANNEL ISLANDS AND THE ISLE OF MAN

In the tenth and eleventh centuries, the Channel Islands (Jersey, Guernsey, Alderney, and Sark are the largest in the group) were part of the Duchy of Normandy; they remained under the control of the English Crown after the loss of mainland Normandy to the French in 1204. Meanwhile, the Isle of Man was under the nominal sovereignty of Norway until 1266; it came under the direct administration of Britain in 1765, when the English government bought it for £70,000.

Today, these territories each have their own legislative assemblies and systems of law, and their own taxation systems, while the United Kingdom is responsible for their international relations and external defense. The Isle of Man's Parliament, Tynwald, established more than a thousand years ago, is the oldest legislature in continuous existence in the world. It is also unique because it has three chambers: the House of Keys; the Legislative Council; and the Tynwald Court, when the House of Keys and the Legislative Council sit together as a single chamber.

from among the members of the House of Commons and, to a lesser extent, the House of Lords. The prime minister is normally the leader of the political party with the most members in the Commons, and the government is dependent on the leading party's support.

Parliament represents the entire country and can legislate for the whole or for any part or combination of parts. The maximum parliamentary term is five years, but the prime minister may ask the monarch to dissolve Parliament and call a general election at any time. The focus of legislative power is the 659-member House of Commons, which has sole jurisdiction over **finance**. The House of Lords, although shorn of most of its powers, can still review, amend, or delay temporarily any bills except those relating to the budget.

In 1999, the government removed the automatic right of hereditary peers to hold seats in the House of Lords. The current house consists of appointed life peers who hold their seats for life and ninety-two **hereditary peers** who will hold their seats only until final reforms have been agreed on and implemented.

The judiciary branch of the government is independent of the legislative and executive branches but cannot review the legitimacy of legislation passed by the legislative branch.

This system of government was born out of Britain's long and ancient history. Today, it is the foundation for the United Kingdom's role in the modern world—and Britain's economy is built on it as well.

London is an international trade center.

CHAPTER 3

THE MODERN-DAY ECONOMY OF THE UNITED KINGDOM

The United Kingdom is one of Europe's great trading powers, and it is also an international finance center. Britain's long years as a world power have also left it with a legacy of influence in the business world. Throughout the twentieth century, it had a strong and thriving *economy*.

Picadilly Circus in London draws a thriving tourist business.

Socialism has been a strong factor in the United Kingdom's economy; in other words, many businesses are public rather than private. The government uses heavy taxes to provide services to all segments of the society, no matter how rich or poor. In the 1980s, however, the government reduced public ownership and put a limit on the growth of social welfare programs. Despite this trend, the Labour Party, which consists of **labor unions** and socialist societies, was able to put its leader, Tony Blair, into the prime minister's office in 1997 with a landslide victory. With the recent recession, however, the UK's government is once again swinging back to the policies of the 1980s, with greater limits on government spending.

QUICK FACTS: THE ECONOMY OF THE UNITED KINGDOM

Gross Domestic Product (GDP): US2.25 trillion (2011 est.)

GDP per capita: $35,900 (2011 est.)

Industries: machine tools, electric power equipment, automation equipment, railroad equipment, shipbuilding, aircraft, motor vehicles and parts, electronics and communications equipment, metals, chemicals, coal, petroleum, paper and paper products, food processing, textiles, clothing, other consumer goods

Agriculture: cereals, oilseed, potatoes, vegetables; cattle, sheep, poultry; fish

Export commodities: manufactured goods, fuels, chemicals; food, beverages, tobacco

Export partners: US 11.4%, Germany 11.2%, Netherlands 8.5%, France 7.7%, Ireland 6.8%, Belgium 5.4% (2010)

Import commodities: manufactured goods, machinery, fuels; foodstuffs

Import partners: Germany 13.1%, China 9.1%, Netherlands 7.5%, France 6.1%, US 5.8%, Norway 5.5%, Belgium 4.9% (2010)

Currency: British pound (GBP)

Currency exchange rate: US$1 = £.6176 (2011)

Note: All figures are from 2011 unless otherwise noted.
Source: www.cia.gov, 2012.

THE FOUNDATION OF BRITAIN'S ECONOMY

The United Kingdom has large coal, natural gas, and oil reserves; these resources provide the economy with a strong foundation. Primary energy production accounts for 10 percent of the **gross domestic product (GDP)**, which is one of the highest percentages of any industrial nation. **Service industries**, particularly banking, insurance, and business services, account for the largest proportion of Britain's GDP, while industry has declined in importance.

Although the United Kingdom is a relatively small island with many urban centers, farming continues to be important to its economy. Its agriculture is highly mechanized and efficient, producing

Scotland's sheep

about 60 percent of its population's food needs with only 1 percent of the nation's labor force. The 1986 discovery of mad cow disease among its beef cattle, however, shook the United Kingdom's farming industry. The nation united with the rest of the EU to take courageous measures to control the crisis, and the UK beef industry is struggling toward recovery.

An Island of Pounds in the Midst of Euros

Most of the EU now uses the euro as its currency—but not the United Kingdom. Former Prime Minister Tony Blair pushed for Britain's conversion, but the nation's good economic performance complicated his government's efforts to make a case for Britain to join the European Economic and Monetary Union (EMU). Critics pointed out that the British economy has done fine outside of the EMU, and public opinion polls showed that a majority of Britons opposed the euro.

The momentum of Britain's thriving economy has pushed it through more than ten years of steady growth, into the twenty-first century. In the early years of the new century, the nation also had lower ***unemployment*** rates than any other industrial nation. What's more, Britain invests more of its money in the United States than any other country does, so its healthy economy also gave jobs to more than a million Americans.

Then, in 2008, the entire world went into a recession—a period when businesses and finance stopped growing. Inflation rose, unemployment increased, and individuals and businesses alike struggled to keep their finances afloat. Because the economies of countries all around the world are so interlinked, especially within the EU, the world's money problems snowballed, becoming worse and worse over the next couple of years.

It works the other way around too, though: as the countries of the world began to grow again, their growth helped one another come out of the recession. Finally, in 2010, the UK's economy began to recover. Businesses did better, and more people had jobs. Growth was slow, however, and economists continued to warn that the UK was in trouble.

Recovery hasn't arrived yet, but the United Kingdom has always been strong. Eventually, its economy will gain back what it lost. More than anything else, its people are what make this nation able to overcome the challenges it faces.

Although many British people now live in cities, there is still a large rural population.

CHAPTER 4 THE UNITED KINGDOM'S PEOPLE AND CULTURE

The people of the United Kingdom are known for their creativity, talent, and industriousness. After all, the British Islands were the birthplace of Newton, Darwin, Shakespeare, the Beatles, Eric Clapton, and the inventors of the hovercraft and the World Wide Web—not to mention J. K. Rowling, the author of the Harry Potter series.

Quick Facts: The People of the United Kingdom

Population: 63,047,162 (July 2012 est.)
Ethnic groups: English 81.5%, Scottish 9.6%, Irish 2.4%, Welsh 1.9%. Ulster 1.8%. West Indian, Indian, Pakistani, and other 2.8%
Age structure:
  0–14 years: 17.3%
  15–64 years: 66.2%
  65 years and over: 16.5% (2011 est.)
Population growth rate: 0.553% (2012 est.)
Birth rate: 12.27 births/1,000 population (2012 est.)
Death rate: 9.33 deaths/1,000 population (July 2012 est.)
Migration rate: 2.59 migrant(s)/1,000 population (2012 est.)
Infant mortality rate: 2.56 deaths/1,000 live births
Life expectancy at birth:
  Total population: 80.17 years
  Male: 78.05 years
  Female: 82.4 years (2012 est.)
Total fertility rate: 1.91 children born/woman (2012 est.)
Religions: Christian (Anglican, Roman Catholic, Presbyterian, Methodist) 71.6%, Muslim 2.7%, Hindu 1%, other 1.6%, unspecified or none 23.1% (2001 census)
Languages: English, Welsh, Scottish form of Gaelic
  note: the following are recognized regional languages: Scots (about 30% of the population of Scotland), Scottish Gaelic (about 60,000 in Scotland), Welsh (about 20% of the population of Wales), Irish (about 10% of the population of Northern Ireland), Cornish (some 2,000 to 3,000 in Cornwall)
Literacy rate: 99% (2000 est.)

Note: All figures are from 2011 unless otherwise noted.
Source: www.cia.gov, 2012.

Population Facts

In 2012, the United Kingdom's population was estimated at more than 63 million, making it one of the largest countries in the EU, and in the world. Its overall population density is also one of the highest on the planet. Almost one-third of the population lives in England's prosperous southeast, with about 7.2 million people in the capital city of London. The British are famous for being reserved in manners, dress, and speech. They are known around the world for their politeness, self-discipline, and their dry sense of humor.

Many of the people of the United Kingdom are descended mainly from the varied ethnic stocks that settled there before the eleventh century. After the Norman invasion, the pre-Celtic, Celtic, Roman, Anglo-Saxon, and Norse influences were blended with the culture of the Scandinavian Vikings who had lived in Northern France. Today Celtic languages persist in Wales, Scotland, and Northern Ireland, but the predominant language is English, a blend of Anglo-Saxon and Norman French.

People in Killin, Scotland, listen to a local band.

A youth hostel near Loch Lomond, Scotland

Modern Britain, however, has attracted immigrants from all over the world, and today it is a country of mixed cultures. London has the largest non-white population of any European city, with over 250 languages spoken there. **Multiculturalism** and a changing economy have gradually worn away the British class system, but features of the system remain.

WHAT IS SOCIAL CLASS?

Sociologists define social class as the grouping of people in terms of wealth or status. In earlier centuries, Great Britain had sharply divided upper and lower classes; the upper class was the nobility, while members of the lower class were referred to as commoners.

In the twentieth century, British society was divided into three main groups: the upper class, the middle class, and the lower or working class. The upper classes tended to consist of people with inherited wealth, and included some of the oldest families, many of whom were aristocrats with titles (such as Sir or Lady). The upper classes were defined by their titles,

RELIGION IN THE UNITED KINGDOM

The Church of England and the Church of Scotland are the official churches in their respective parts of the country, but because the United Kingdom has such a large immigrant population, most religions found in the world are represented in the United Kingdom.

but also by their education and their pastimes, which included the traditional sports hunting, shooting, fishing, and horseback riding. The middle classes made up the majority of the population of Britain and included industrialists, professionals, businesspeople, and shop owners. Meanwhile, working-class people were mostly farm, mine, and factory workers. The British could tell which class people belonged to by their accent, by their clothes, by the way that they educated their children, and even by their interests and the types of food they ate.

In today's United Kingdom, however, class is more apt to be based on occupation. From this perspective, doctors, lawyers, and university teachers are given more status than unskilled laborers. The different positions

Did You Know?
Famous Authors from the United Kingdom
William Shakespeare
Charlotte Brontë
Emily Brontë
Jane Austen
Robert Burns
William Wordsworth
Lewis Carroll
Elizabeth Barrett Browning
Charles Dickens
Agatha Christie
J. R. R. Tolkien
J. K. Rowling

represent different levels of power, influence, and money.

A NATION OF TRADITIONS

From Scotland to England, from Northern Ireland to the Channel Islands, the people of Great Britain love customs and traditions. Here are some of the strangest, oldest, and most interesting.

TOSSING BREAD AND CHEESE

On Whit Sunday Evening, after the evening service at the church in St. Braivels, Gloucestershire, basketfuls of bread and cheese are thrown from a wall near the old castle. Everyone scrambles to grab as many pieces of food as they can. The locals of St. Braivels have been throwing bread and cheese since the thirteenth century, when the custom began, probably as a payment for the villagers' right to cut timber from a nearby wood.

PIES AND BOTTLE RUGBY

According to an old story, hundreds of years ago a woman was saved by a hare running across the path of a bull on Easter Monday in Hallaton in Leicestershire. As a token of her appreciation, she gave a piece of land to the rector, with the request that the rector have a hare pie made to be distributed to parishioners together with a large quantity of ale every year.

THE BRITISH ISLES' FAIRIES, PIXIES, AND BROWNIES

From Arthurian legends to children's stories, from Shakespeare to Disney, from garden gnomes to greeting cards, magical beings are an integral part of Western culture. For hundreds of years, these creatures have inhabited the hills and moors of the British Isles.

Some say these creatures have their roots in actual history. When the Anglo-Saxon invaders came to the British Isles, they pushed the smaller, earlier inhabitants back into the hills, into their burrows and caves. One group was called the Picts, small people who painted their skin blue. Linguistic experts have pointed to the similarities between the word "pixie" and "Pict."

The United Kingdom today is an ultramodern and multicultural nation—and yet many of its people still believe in the existence of fairies. During the 1990s, for example, when a government-sponsored program expanded roadways at the same time that private industries were extending open quarries, protesters against these actions came to regard themselves as aided by fairies in a cause that pitted nature against human destruction, the little people against the much larger and corrupt forces of modern society.

Britain's fairies and the other inhabitants of their enchanted world have inspired the human imagination for over a thousand years—and they continue to do so today.

Ancient traditions linger in U.K. villages.

A cricket game

The hare pie (replaced now by a beef pie) is still produced at the church gate, and pieces are hurled to a good-natured mob, who then make a procession led by a bronze sculpture of a hare, before the start of a rugby-like game between Hallaton and nearby Medbourne. The aim is to get bottles (three small iron-hooped wooden barrels) across streams that are a mile apart.

CHEESE ROLLING

This event takes place in different parts of the country, usually on the Spring Bank Holiday Monday. A round cheese hurtles down a nearly vertical slope, chased by competitors. The winner is the first person to grab the cheese. It is spectacular to watch, but many competitors end up with broken arms and legs.

The National Anthem of the United Kingdom God Save the Queen

(the same tune as "My Country, 'Tis of Thee")

God save our gracious Queen,
Long live our noble Queen,
God save the Queen!
Send her victorious,
Happy and glorious,
Long to reign over us,
God save the Queen!

BRITISH SPORTS

The British are famous for their sports, including cricket and rugby. The game of golf is popularly believed to have been invented in Scotland, though other countries have recently laid claims to its origins.

EDUCATION

The United Kingdom is a nation steeped in tradition—but it is also very much a part of the twenty-first century, thanks in large part to the excellence of its educational system. The nation's high **literacy rate** (99 percent) can be credited to the **universal** public education introduced for the primary level in 1870 and the secondary level in 1900. Today, education is mandatory from ages five through sixteen, and about one-fifth of British students go on to postsecondary education.

The people of the United Kingdom have an ancient and rich culture that is being enhanced today by people from all over the world. As the nation looks to the future, it is building on the strengths and knowledge of many cultures.

Did You Know? Famous Musical Composers from the United Kingdom
William Byrd
Thomas Tallis
John Taverner
Henry Purcell
Edward Elgar
Arthur Sullivan
Ralph Vaughan
   Williams
Benjamin Britten
John Lennon
Paul McCartney

London's skyline at night

5 LOOKING TO THE FUTURE

The United Kingdom may no longer be the world power it was during the nineteenth century, but as it looks forward into the years to come, it nevertheless plans to take an active role on the world stage. The UK's influence is felt around the world, and the British plan on keeping it that way.

At the same time, though, the UK knows it has challenges it must face in the twenty-first century. Although these are modern problems, many of them have their roots in Britain's past.

NORTHERN IRELAND

When Ireland became independent in 1921, the six northern, mostly Protestant counties remained part of the United Kingdom and became known as Northern Ireland. Not everyone was happy about this arrangement. The pro-Catholic Irish Republican Army (IRA) waged a **terrorist campaign** to reunite the two areas of Ireland.

In 1999, After years of difficult **negotiations**, the Good Friday Agreement brought together both Catholics and Protestants under a government led by an elected executive committee. But the years of conflict could not be resolved quickly or simply. Continued uncertainty over the future of Northern Ireland has held back the region's economy, as few companies are willing to invest in the area. Unemployment in Northern Ireland is the highest in the United Kingdom.

Fences and walls separating Protestants and Catholics are visible reminders that the scars of the past still remain. In 2011, Justice Minister David Ford said, "These walls, fences and gates are daily reminders that despite the political progress we have made over the last decade, we still have a huge challenge ahead to break down the mistrust and separation that exists within our community. Building a shared future is not an optional extra—it goes to the core of transform-ing society and building a new Northern Ireland in which people can live, learn and work together in safety. . . . We must create partnerships at both political and community levels so that together we can start the process of removing these physical reminders of separation."

THE ENVIRONMENT AND ENERGY

The United Kingdom is also committed to the planet's future. Its government has set policy goals that include cutting the UK's carbon dioxide **emissions** by 80 percent by 2050, with an in-between target between 26 percent and 32 percent by 2020. This goal was passed into law in 2008, making the United Kingdom the first country in the world to set such a long-range and significant carbon reduction target within such a legally binding framework. The UK also supports the EU taking a strong role in reducing carbon dioxide emissions around the world.

For years, the UK has relied on coal and off-shore gas supplies for most of its energy, but its people are worried that their nation, like the rest of the world, is increasingly dependent on foreign oil. The UK hopes to change that. The government's goal for renewable energy production is to produce 20 percent of electricity in the UK by the year 2020.

The UK has other environmental goals it plans to achieve by 2020:

• Over 1.2 million people will be employed in green jobs.

The United Kingdom is trying to lower its dependency on foreign oil.

- The efficiency of 7 million homes will have been upgraded, with over 1.5 million of them generating renewable energy.

- Forty percent of electricity will be generated from low-carbon sources, with 30 percent coming from renewable energy sources and another 10 percent from nuclear power and clean coal.

- Gasoline imports will be 50 percent lower.

- The average new car will emit 40 percent less carbon compared to 2009 levels.

At the same time, the British government is working hard to convert to biofuels for its cars and trucks.

AN AGING POPULATION

Another problem confronting the United Kingdom is its aging population: more and more people in the UK are old, while fewer and fewer are young adults and children. As the elderly population of the country continues to expand, the country has a growing need for younger workers to fill jobs. The aging population will also place strains on the country's already overburdened **social security system**.

Older people in the UK, as well as people there who have fallen on hard times, worry about the ways their country is changing. For more than fifty years, the UK has been a socialist nation that took care of its people when they were sick, old, or facing hardships. But since the recession of 2008, the UK government (like many other nations within the EU) has also fallen on hard times—and as a result, many of the nation's public services are being changed and often cut. Older people wonder if they will have an income in their old age, and they worry that they will not have the services they need to stay healthy. The British government is working hard to find the answers it needs to solve this crisis.

THE UNITED KINGDOM AND THE EU

British leaders have stated that their nation plans to play a strong and positive role within the European Union in the years to come, working to ensure that all the nations of Europe are equipped to face the challenges of the twenty-first century, especially in regards to global competitiveness, global warming, and global poverty.

At the same time, the British government is committed to being accountable to its people for what it does on their behalf in the EU. Government leader William Hague has stated, "We will play our role [in the EU] with enthusiasm while vigorously advancing our country's interests."

The British people have a long, strong history. They will need to build on that strength as they face the challenges the future holds.

Time Line

55 BCE   Julius Caesar invades the British Isles.

43 CE   Romans bring the British Isles into the Roman Empire.

330   Pytheas becomes the first person who can read and write to visit the British Isles.

410   Roman Empire withdraws from Britain.

597   St. Augustine comes to Britain as a missionary from Rome.

1066   William, Duke of Normandy, sails across the English Channel and conquers the Anglo-Saxons.

1215   King John is forced to sign the Magna Carta.

1485   Wars of the Roses ends.

1620   Pilgrims set out for the "New World."

1765   United Kingdom buys the Isle of Man.

1837   Queen Victoria assumes the throne.

1870   Universal public education is introduced for the primary level; it is extended to secondary level in 1900.

1919   Irish Republic Army begins operation.

1921   Northern Ireland is allowed to have its own Parliament; Southern Ireland breaks from the United Kingdom and becomes the Republic of Ireland.

1959   Britain joins in the creation of the European Free Trade Association.

1973   Britain joins the European Community.

1979   Margaret Thatcher becomes the first woman prime minister of Britain.

1998   Britain serves as president of the European Union.

1999   British government removes the automatic right of hereditary peer to serve in Parliament.
The Good Friday Agreement brings an official end to the conflict in Northern Ireland.

2004   The EU expands to include Eastern European nations.

2008   Recession hits the entire world.
Britain passes a law committing the UK to a challenging plan for reducing carbon emissions by 2050.

2012   The UK continues to experience an economic slowdown that teeters on recession.

FIND OUT MORE

Allan, Tony. *Troubles in Northern Ireland*. Portsmouth, N.H.: Heinemann, 2004.

Heath, Robin. *Stonehenge*. New York: Walker and Company, 2002.

Hole, Abigail, Etain O'Carroll, and John King. *Wales*. Clerkenwell, London, U.K.: Lonely Planet Publications, 2004.

Innes, Brian. *United Kingdom*. Chicago, Ill.: Raintree, 2002.

Lace, William W. *Scotland*. Farmington Hills, Mich.: Thomson Gale, 2000.

Travel Information
www.visitbritain.com
www.i-uk.com

History and Geography
www.bbc.co.uk/history
www.britannia.com

Culture and Festivals
www.woodlands-junior.kent.sch.uk/customs/questions
www.letsgo.com/132-great_britain-travel-guides-england-d

Economic and Political Information
www.cia.gov/library/publications/the-world-factbook/geos/uk.html

EU Information
europa.eu.int/

GLOSSARY

affirmation: A formal declaration.

arbitrary: Based solely on personal wishes, feelings, or perceptions.

autonomous: Able to act independently.

autonomy: Political independence and self-government.

Axis: The military and political alliance of Germany, Italy, and eventually Japan that fought the Allies in World War II.

bailiffs: People whose jobs it is to carry out the law.

campaign: An organized course of action to achieve a particular goal.

charter members: Founding or original members of a society or organization.

civil wars: Wars between opposing groups within a country.

common law: The body of law that developed as a result of custom and judicial decisions rather than from legislative measures.

Depression: The period of high unemployment, low economic activity, and widespread poverty that occurred between 1929 and 1939.

discrimination: Unfair and unequal treatment of people based on their race, culture, religion, sex, appearance, or some other quality.

economy: The wealth and resources of a country.

emissions: The production and discharge of gas, radiation, or other pollution.

empire: A group of nations, territories, or peoples ruled by a single authority, especially an emperor or empress.

evicted: Forced to leave

finance: The management of large amounts of money.

gross domestic product (GDP): The total value of all goods and services produced within a country in a year.

hereditary peers: Descendents who hold titles based on heredity.

inflation: An increase in the price of goods and services.

intimidated: Frightened someone in order to make them do something.

labor unions: Organizations that are set up to serve and advance their members' interests in terms of wages, benefits, working hours, and working conditions.

literacy rate: The percentage of people who can read and write at a competent level.

moors: Large, uncultivated, treeless stretches of land covered with bracken, heather, coarse grasses, or moss.

multiculturalism: The existence of cultures of different countries, ethnic groups, or religions.

national sovereignty: The ability of a country to be free from outside interference and to be able to self-govern.

nationalism: A feeling of intense loyalty to one's country.

negotiations: Discussions intended to build an agreement between two groups.

nobles: Those belonging to an aristocratic social or political class.

pensions: Retirement payments.

racism: The belief that all members of a particular race share the same characteristics, especially negative characteristics.

recession: A period when businesses and finances produce less.

service industries: Industries that provide a service rather than goods.

social security system: A government plan that helps people who lack money, especially those who are elderly or disabled.

socialism: A political and economic theory that says the production, distribution, and sale of goods should be owned or regulated by the community as a whole.

sociologists: Scientists who study the origin, development, and structure of human societies and the behavior of individuals and groups in society.

terrorist: Having to do with a group that takes action specifically intended to terrify people as a way to make people do what the group wants.

unemployment: Lack of jobs.

universal: Available to all.

INDEX

PICTURE CREDITS

Benjamin Stewart, Harding House Publishing Services, took all photographs with the following exceptions:

Pg 10 © fazon - Fotolia.com
Pg 57 © lightmoon - Fotolia.com

About the Authors and the Consultant

Authors

Shaina Carmel Indovino is a writer and illustrator living in Nesconset, New York. She graduated from Binghamton University, where she received degrees in sociology and English. Shaina has enjoyed the opportunity to apply both of her fields of study to her writing and she hopes readers will benefit from taking a look at the countries of the world world through more than one perspective.

Rae Simons has written several nonfiction children's books, as well as children's and adult fiction. Her grandparents came to the United States from the United Kingdom, and she has always loved learning about British history and culture.

Series Consultant

Ambassador John Bruton served as Irish Prime Minister from 1994 until 1997. As prime minister, he helped turn Ireland's economy into one of the fastest-growing in the world. He was also involved in the Northern Ireland Peace Process, which led to the 1998 Good Friday Agreement. During his tenure as Ireland's prime minister, he also presided over the European Union presidency in 1996 and helped finalize the Stability and Growth Pact, which governs management of the euro. Before being named the European Commission Head of Delegation in the United States, he was a member of the convention that drafted the European Constitution, signed October 29, 2004.

The European Commission Delegation to the United States represents the interests of the European Union as a whole, much as ambassadors represent their countries' interests to the U.S. government. Matters coming under European Commission authority are negotiated between the commission and the U.S. administration.